Reading M[...]

Contents

A Classroom 2

A Playground 4

A Neighborhood 6

Over the Highways 8

Over Land and Water 10

North America 12

The Earth 14

David Rhys

A Classroom

Maps and photographs can show us the same
places, but they show them in different ways.
This is a photograph of a classroom. You can see
tables, chairs, computers, two walls, a door,
and children.

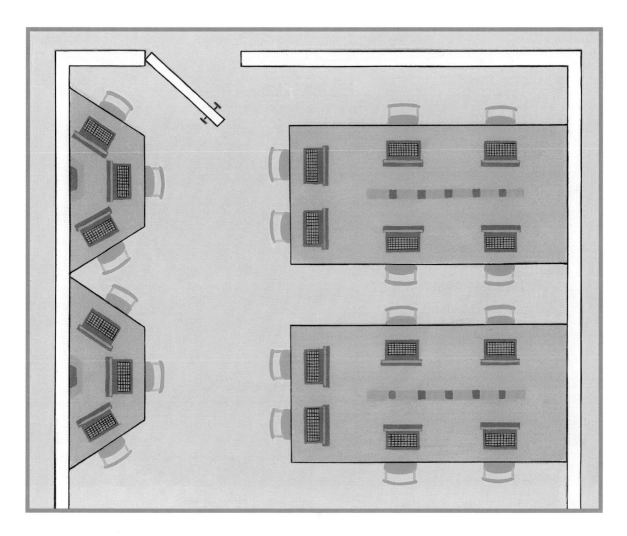

This is a map of the same classroom. You can see the tables, chairs, and computers. You can see three walls and a door. The only things missing are the children.

A Playground

This is a photograph of a playground. You can see the path to the playground, benches, steps, a bridge, platforms, and sand.

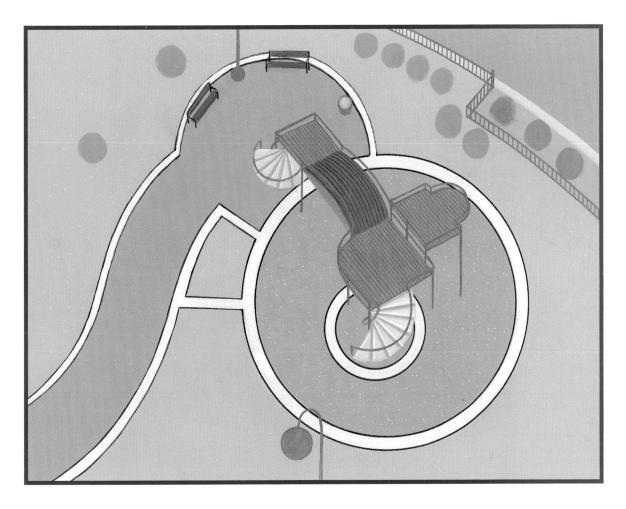

This is a map of the same playground. Find the benches. What else do you see?

A Neighborhood

This is a photograph of houses in a neighborhood.
The photo was taken by a person in a helicopter.
This kind of photo is called a bird's-eye view.
It's how a bird might see the houses.

This is a map of the same houses in the same neighborhood. Most maps show a bird's-eye view. They show what a place looks like from above.

Over the Highways

This photo is a bird's-eye view of two highways.
You can see roads, an overpass, a river, and a
bridge. The photo was taken from an airplane.

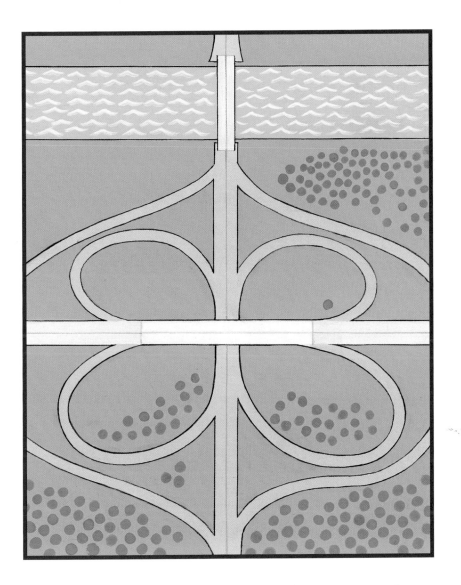

This is a map of the same place. Look at
the photograph again. Why do the cars
on the highway look so small?

Over Land and Water

This is a photo of San Francisco taken from a satellite in space. The satellite was so high that the photo does not show cars or houses or even big buildings. But you do see land and water.

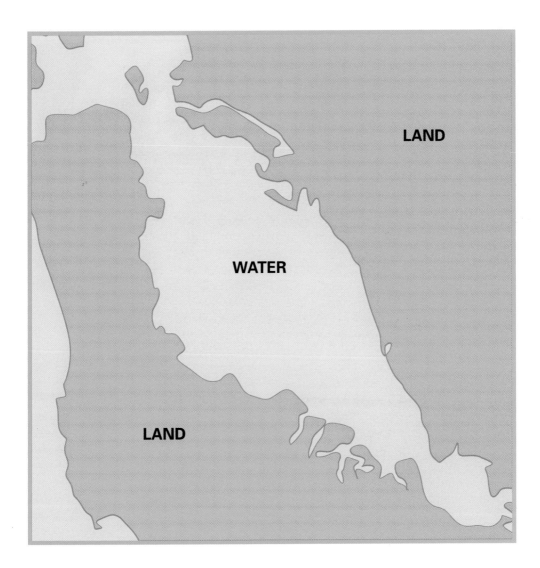

This is a map of the same area. There are labels for land and water.

North America

This is a photograph of North America taken from space. You can see snow and ice. You can see the mountains in Canada, the United States, and Mexico.

This is a map of North America. This map shows countries and oceans. It does not show snow and mountains, but you know where they are.

The Earth

This is a photograph of our planet Earth taken from space. It shows North America and South America and the oceans around them.

This is called a globe. It is a model of planet Earth. This side shows the same area that the photograph shows.

Remember that every map is a picture. It shows a part of our world.